Sandra Green was born in 1948, in a small village in North Yorkshire. Sandra is the youngest of four children.

Throughout her life, she has achieved copious amounts of life experiences, which have opened many doors. Sandra spent the majority of her employment in accounting; however, she also ran her own pub and travelled worldwide.

In 2009, Sandra was diagnosed with Parkinson's disease. This inspired her to start writing in a bid to help raise extra funds for the local Parkinson's group. Furthermore, her passion for life and love of poetry has led her to creating her own beautiful book of poems.

This book is dedicated to all the wonderful people I have had the pleasure of sharing life's journey with.

Sandra Green

THE POEMS OF SANDRA GREEN

AUSTIN MACAULEY PUBLISHERS™
LONDON * CAMBRIDGE * NEW YORK * SHARJAH

Copyright © Sandra Green 2022

The right of Sandra Green to be identified as author of this work has been asserted by the author in accordance with section 77 and 78 of the Copyright, Designs and Patents Act 1988.

All rights reserved. No part of this publication may be reproduced, stored in a retrieval system, or transmitted in any form or by any means, electronic, mechanical, photocopying, recording, or otherwise, without the prior permission of the publishers.

Any person who commits any unauthorised act in relation to this publication may be liable to criminal prosecution and civil claims for damages.

A CIP catalogue record for this title is available from the British Library.

ISBN 9781398457706 (Paperback)
ISBN 9781398457713 (ePub e-book)

www.austinmacauley.com

First Published 2022
Austin Macauley Publishers Ltd®
1 Canada Square
Canary Wharf
London
E14 5AA

I would like to take this opportunity to acknowledge the people who have helped me to create my book of poems. My children Michael and Carolyn who make me proud to be their mum, my three grandsons and my late partner Arthur.

Alpbach

I arrive in Alpbach on a lovely May day
It is the flower village of Austria, they say
I know the European Forum is held here every year
But my guests will be looking forward to a nice cold beer.

We meet in the village the next day
Where I show them the path that we will take
To reach the white speck you see between the trees
It's the Bischofer Arms, where we have a Tiroler Grodtlosel to eat.

Everyone is having fun trying to do the traditional dance
The men wearing ladaer hosen are a wonderful sight
And the ladies have on dirndi dresses that are a delight
They look gorgeous in the evening moonlight.

Time goes so fast and the coach is here
The guests wave goodbye saying, 'We will be back next year.'
I go to the hotels and check that the new bookings are right
The new guests will be arriving on the very next flight.

Sandra Green

Catwalk

Come on now, girls, give us a twirl,
Let's see you strut your stuff
That's what they say, is it not?
So on to the catwalk you go
Start the music, Joe.

The girls are fantastic
They look gorgeous in those hats,
And that, my dear Florence, is a fact.
The customers, I think, are enjoying the show
Let's hope we get plenty of orders before they go.

Well, girls, what can I say,
You were absolutely marvellous today
Therefore, you will receive a bonus in this week's pay.
The customers gave lots of compliments and orders galore
So now we are having Champagne to celebrate
And my feet can once again touch the floor.

Sandra Green

Coronavirus

My daughter's getting worried
She is trying to hold me down,
'Mum, keep still,' she says with a frown.
'I have sent for an ambulance
They will be here soon
This Coronavirus is making you weird
It's just not you.'

I wake up in the hospital
Not remembering a thing
When told what I said and did,
How embarrassing.
So least said the better
That's what they say
I can tell that story another day.

Here comes the doctor making his rounds
He says I'm a lot better, so homeward bound.
The next two weeks are spent in isolation
Then a letter arrives stating a date for my vaccination.
Everything seems to be on hold and taking time
Oh how I want to hug those grandsons of mine.

Sandra Green

Dark Nights

It is so cold but no movement must I make
Deep growls fill the night's silence
Do I run for my life or stay?
There really isn't any option
My mind's made up; run, but which way?

Out of breath, I stand with my back against a tree
I see something moving very slowly
With bright eyes and bearing its teeth
It's coming towards me, oh no
Time to run again, I must flee.

The snow continues to fall; I trip, down the slope I go
Putting my arms and legs out to save myself
I wake up in bed, clutching my head
Realising that I was dreaming about the film I saw on TV
I decided to get up and make a drink of tea.

Sandra Green

Dreaming of Peace

Oh to spread my wings
And fly away to another land
Where I can be myself
For once make my stand.

I dream of the day to come
When peace will enter my life
No longer feeling the urge to run
Away from all this strife.

May be this will only come in time
When I take my last breath and die
Leaving everything behind
No more to cry for lost time.

Sandra Green

Ducking-Stool

In days gone by, a woman would cry
If accused of abusive language
The magistrate would choose which
Punishment to use, the bridle or the ducking-stool.

Usually, the pond was dirty and deep
If they were lucky, the mud would only touch their feet
But after been dunked several times whilst being strapped down
They would swallow the water and eventually drowned.

The ducking-stool was used for eight centuries
In every parish and market town
It was used by the House of Correction
At Liverpool in the year 1799.

Sandra Green

Foxy Loxy

I look at the clock;
It is half past two in the morning
And I'm finding it difficult to go back to sleep
So I decide to get up and make a drink of tea
Should I have a biscuit, why not two or three?

I sit watching the trees and flowers swaying gently in the breeze
When all of a sudden, I see a fox baring his teeth
Now the fox is rolling in the grass, oh I would love a photo of that
But if I made a sound, he would go to ground fast.

He is on the prowl again; I don't know what he has seen
Maybe it's a mouse, but whatever it is, it's now in his mouth
And as he quickly goes back to his lair
His big bushy tail is swishing about in the air.

Sandra Green

From Out of the Darkness

From out of the darkness comes an eerie sound
But no one seems to care as they stand around
I hold my mother's hand tight and cling to her side
As more people arrive, I just want to hide.

The ground under my feet seems to vibrate
As the sound grows louder I begin to shake
When I look into the darkness, now a glow appears
It's definitely getting closer and it's just as I feared.

Everyone surges forward so you make your stand
'Please get back from the edge,' comes the command
The monster arrives and gobbles everyone up in a flash
We are on the underground train going home at last.

Sandra Green

Henry the Hedgehog

The leaves moved very slowly on the ground

Whatever it was, did not make a sound
Benjamin watched closely, whispering, 'What have I found?'
A little black nose first came into sight
Then two little eyes, looking very bright
Could it be next door's cat?
No, it's a hedgehog; he's got spikes on his back.

Benjamin was thinking, as the hedgehog sniffed the air
'I must give you a name,' he declared
'Brian, George, Jeffery, Jack
No, I can't call you that
I know, Henry! That sounds just right
Now let me see, when do you eat
Is it during the day or night?'

Just then, Benjamin heard his mum calling his name
'My tea's ready, Henry, what a shame.'
As Benjamin turned to leave, what did he discover
A larger hedgehog, 'You must be his mother.'
On hearing his voice, they rolled into a ball

'Are you frightened because I'm so tall?
Oh please, stay in my garden, I will be back soon
With a saucer of water and a little food.'

An hour later, Benjamin returned to the garden
And walked over to the side
Carrying a box of straw that was open on one side
And putting it down carefully, so as not to spill their drink,
He laid some bread crumbs on the ground
Then sat and waited, not making a sound
Thinking to himself, *Has this been a waste of time?*

Benjamin was just about to go; 'Time for bed,' shouted his brother
When all of a sudden, he saw Henry appear with his mother
They walked slowly, eating the bread crumbs that they found
Making their way to the box that was on the ground
Henry went in and drank some water, followed by his mother
This is fantastic! thought Benjamin, *I must go and tell my brothers.*
He crept down the garden path and then ran into the house
'Matthew, James, come see my hedgehogs, but be as quiet as a mouse.'

'I'm sorry, Benjamin,' said Mum, 'the boys are getting ready for bed
So up the stairs you go and tell them about Fred.'
'His name is not Fred, it is Henry and his mother.'
'Well, I am sure they will be in our garden again tomorrow.'
'Oh, I do hope so, Mum, it has been fun today,
I can give them more food to eat and straw for where they lay.'
'To bed now, please, I will be upstairs soon, to kiss you goodnight.'
Benjamin was ready for bed and fast asleep in the blink of an eye.

Sandra Green

I Know You Cannot Hear Me

I know you cannot hear my voice,
Or see my smile any more,
But I will be beside you,
Just as I was before.

I will listen to your stories and wipe away your tears,
You will feel my arm around you,
And help to calm your fears.

I know I'm not visible to see you with my eyes,
But I will still talk to you in silence,
And my spirit will reply.

You will feel the love I have for you,
You will hear my words in your heart,
Although I have no body,
Our souls will never part.

Sandra Green

It's a Dog's Life

'Come on into the car,' they say
'We are in a terrible hurry
It's time we were on our way
Jump up now, Ben, that's a good boy
Look, we have your favourite toy.'

'Are we all going out for the day?'
I wag my tail in anticipation
And get into the car without hesitation
But as we set off, little James pats my head
Asking his dad, 'Did you remember Ben's bed?'

The car comes to a stop, 'Out you get,' James says
He gives me a hug, 'Don't worry, Ben
It will only be for two weeks and a day.'
My lead is put into the hands of a stranger
'You can't leave me here, I could be in danger.'
I sit and watch as they drive away
Howling loudly, and looking very sad
'What have I done to deserve this, have I been bad?'
'Come now, Ben,' the lady strokes my back,
'Let's go for a walk along the old cycle path.'

'Jack and Tess, meet Ben, who has also come to stay
Walk together nicely now, you'll have lots of time to play.'
Well, maybe this place isn't so bad after all.
Everyone seems happy as they run and fetch the ball
Maybe my planning to escape can wait.

How many days have passed, I'm not sure
But laying on the rug at night by Julie's feet
Contented, tummy full of food and treats
Tied from all the games we have played
I wonder did I really plan to run away?

Playing in the garden with Fraser
Who arrived last night and cried for hours
Now having fun jumping all over the flowers
Julie and Charlotte don't seem to mind
As out of their pockets, treats are found.

I recognised the sound of a car that's just arrived
Here comes James running up the drive
'Oh Ben! I have missed you,' he says
'Come on, boy, you are going home today.'
Well, I suppose I should go and lick his face.

I run back to Julie and Charlotte to say goodbye
Rubbing their legs with my head and give a cry
Let's hope they go on holiday again next year
Then if I'm lucky, they will bring me back here
James calls me again and I jump into the car
Don't worry, Ben, it's not very far.

Oh yes, this is what I call a dog's life.

Sandra Green

Joseph Smith

People would come from miles around
To watch Joseph Smith fell chimneys to the ground
If a Steeple-Jack was required
Then he was the one to hire.

But he sometimes made people horrified
Like when he fell off a ladder that was twenty-five foot high
Everyone thought he would be dead
But no, they found him sitting on the floor holding his head.

The most hazardous job he did was
To attach a flag to the lance of St. George
That was sixty-five foot tall
And stood on the spire of the old Rochdale Town Hall.

Sandra Green

Just One More Step

One more step, that's all it takes
Easy to say but hard to make
Stumbling around and trying not to fall
Feeling embarrassed as I again stop and stall.

The driver of the car coming towards me slows down
He keeps waving me across the road and starts to frown
But he does not understand, my feet don't want to move
I wish that I could make him see that I am not a fool.

At last, my feet begin to move but only on the spot
But now I know it's just a matter of time before I can shut off
Oh thank goodness I am moving and across the road I go, into the shopping
precinct where it doesn't matter if I'm slow.

Sandra Green

Memories

He would spend hours in the garden
And much to his delight
Passers-by would comment
"What a beautiful sight!"
The grass cut and edged with precision
With colourful flowers all around
This was better than working underground.

He had worked down the mines
Until it was time to retire
Digging for coal in the darkness
To light our fires
A beam of light shining from his helmet
As he worked through the night
Showering at five, then home to Mary, his wife.
He loved watching westerns
Sitting in his favourite chair by the fire
A drink of tea by his side
John Wayne saying, "It was time to ride,"
But should I have a problem or needed his advice
He would listen quietly, his eyes gentle and bright
Solving what troubled me, making everything right.

Oh how I loved my dad, so special was he
The holidays when we were young
Were full of laughter and lots of fun
And Mum was happy sitting on the beach
As we played in the sun and paddling in the sea

Building castles with our buckets and spades
Until it was time to get ready for tea.

Memories are all that I have left of you
There was no time to say goodbye
You left us so suddenly, oh how I cried
After all, you were far too young to die
And now I look at your photo, with your lovely smile
And remember all the good times we had
I love and miss you, Dad.

                                                Sandra Green

Miss Dee

I've been picked at last
The lady is asking
"How much for that cat?"
The shopkeeper wants twenty pounds
But on hearing this, the lady frowns
"Come now, it is only an ordinary cat,
I will give you ten pounds, no more than that."

The shopkeeper grumbles to himself
As he plucks me from my cage
And the lady hands him a basket
Saying, "Now that should keep him safe."
I don't hesitate, escaping from his grip
Meowing loudly, I jump into the lady's arms
And start to purr, as she gives him her ten pounds.

"Let's get you settled in the car,
We will be home soon, it's not very far."
She strokes my back, as into the basket I go

"We will think of a name for you before we arrive home."
As she drives down the road, I hear her mumble, "Maybe Ted,
No, that's not you, but neither is Fred,
I know, we will call you Henry," and I purr in delight.

Well, what more could I ask for as I look at my bed
She sure knows how to make me happy, I'm glad she didn't call me Fred,
Henry sounds quite nice as I hear my name called
Arriving in the kitchen, I find my mistress holding a bowl
"Come now, Henry, have something to eat and drink."
This is definitely the life to lead, don't you think?
I have eaten and drank my milk and now curled up on her knee
Oh this is wonderful; my life is now complete, thanks to Miss Dee.

Sandra Green

My Little Garden Friend

Here he comes to stand next to me
To see what I have found,
As I dig between the flowers
A worm appears in the ground.

Mr Robin does not hesitate
He grabs the worm in his beak
And flies off to his nest, where
There are young mouths to feed.

Back he comes to join me
And tilts his head to one side
As much as to say
'Get digging, time's passing by.'

'I need feeding, too, Robin
So let's sit on the grass for our lunch.
Here is bread for you and your crew
That should make for one happy bunch.'

Sandra Green

My Love

I visit my love and find him staring into space,
But he doesn't recognise me as I bend to kiss his face.
I wish that he was better and we could be together again,
Unfortunately, that will never happen; I must accept what has been planned.

In the past, we would spend ages in the garden
Arthur mowing the lawn and I looking after the flowers,
Then we would sit under the umbrella talking for hours
About what we would do when we retired.

I dream at night that he is by my side,
His arms wrapped around me holding me tight,
But when I awake in the morning, alone and whisper his name
I know that our lives will never be the same.

He is my love and my best friend
I wish with all my heart that this nightmare would end,
Giving us time together with lots of laughter and no pain
Just the two of us enjoying life again.

Sandra Green

One Last Chance

All that I ask is one last chance
Is that too much to ask?
I should have found the time to care
After all that you gave to me
Your time and bounteous love
You were always there
When I needed you.

Please, oh please, don't go
It's too soon, I need more time
To tell you everything
That is on my mind
To ask for your forgiveness
For all the mistakes I have made
Oh how my heart aches.

Can you hear me, Mum
Please try to give me a sign
A squeeze of my hand
Or a blink of your eyes
This is my last chance to say
I love you so much in so many ways
My wonderful, precious mum.

Sandra Green

Plague Stones

In days gone by when the plague was rife
County folk thought money was the source of infection
So when they sold their wares
It was with care
Outside of the city walls
Where they could breathe the air.

At the end of the day
The money was taken away
And put into a large plague stone
That was sometimes called a penny stone
It would contain vinegar to kill any germs
Before taking it home.

The vinegar was put into the stone
that was shaped inside like a cup
and two stones can be found at Lancaster.
One on the road from the south
and one upon the north road.

                                        Sandra Green

Reminiscing

I close my eyes and see you standing near the fire
A glass of whisky in one hand and a cigarette in the other
We would smooch to the music playing softly in the back ground
And in the early hours, when you fell asleep on the couch
I would cover you up and leave without making a sound.

Driving home, I would play music that sometimes made me cry
I loved you so very much but time was passing me by
So I decided to work abroad to get you out of my mind
But with your photo by my bedside and your phone calls late at night
You asked me to return and live with you, no more to take flight.

Twenty-four years have gone by so fast
Why, oh why did he take you? I ask
We had so much planed for when we retired
Going on the motorbike for hours and hours
Visiting our children and taking them flowers.

I look at your photos and tell you what is planned for the day
And when it is time for bed, good night I say
I feel your arms around me holding me tight
Is this real or am I dreaming, it's late and dark outside
So once again I say good night and turn out the light.

Sandra Green

Samuel

That wonderful smile that lights up his face,
He tells you a tale at a fantastic pace,
With dark brown eyes, full of mischief,
That pulls the strings of your heart,
From the moment you meet him
To the time that you part.

'Come on, let's play football,' he shouts.
As he makes for the stairs,
'You can be in goals first, Nana,' he declares.
We play for a while until another game takes his eye
Toy cars and motorbikes go racing by
He sings to himself as he happily plays
Oh how much love he gives in so many ways.

                                                                                            Sandra Green

Sayings

Where do the sayings come from, I would really like to know
For intense, I have more than one string to my bow
Or, burying your head in the sand
We know what is implied, but who dreamt them up
He or she must have had a very unusual mind.

Come on now, hurry up, don't delay
Time waits for no man, my mother would say,
There's no smoke without fire and
I have eyes in the back of my head
That one I didn't want to hear and would always dread.

It's good luck if a black cat crosses your path
But don't cross on the stairs or stand on a crack
It just depends on what you believe and your ways
So who did make them up and for why, do tell
For I have just broken a mirror, will this mean seven years of hell?

Sandra Green

Stiletto Shoes

It's lovely when we reminisce about all the crazy things we did
When we would dance around the room
Elvis singing 'Blue Suede' Shoes on the gramophone
Putting our makeup on, using the mirror over the fire
Back combing our hair getting it higher and higher
"How much longer are you going to be?" Dad would say
"Blocking my view of the TV, would you please get out of the way?"

On with our stilettoes, we were ready to rock and roll
However did we dance in those shoes I'll never know,
The Dave Clark Five, The Animals and other groups would play
Around the room the guys would stand
Plucking up the courage to ask, "Do you want to dance?"
And most of the time, we replied, "Not a chance."
Those were the good old days.

Remember how quickly the night would go by and you would say,
"It's time to put our coats on, hurry up now, don't delay."
Rushing to catch the last bus home, you could always hear the sound

Of our stiletto heels tip tapping on the ground
Home at last, we take off our shoes and creep into the house
Then up to bed we would go being as quiet as a mouse
And whisper goodnight.

Sandra Green

Tears of Joy

The waiting is unbearable but there's excitement in the air,
Come now, hurry this way please, the nurse declares.
I rush to see my son holding a baby in his arms,
He proudly announces, 'It's a boy
with my looks and his mother's charms.'

He's perfect, he's gorgeous with blond hair and blue eyes,
Tears of joy run down my cheeks as he yawns and gives a little cry.
How can I explain in words my feelings that lay deep within
Of becoming a grandma for the very first time and
Knowing the happiness this baby will bring.

Sandra Green

The Devil Upon the Dun Horse

Once upon a time there was tailor, who drank and frittered his money away
He would rely on his wife to beg and provide food for the day
Whilst drinking and getting maudlin at his local inn
A stranger came amongst his friends, who kept gazing at him
Feeling uneasy, the tailor decided to make his way home
Walking briskly along, he nervously looked around, for he didn't feel alone
Suddenly, a bright light shone down and the stranger materialised
Granted the tailor three wishes, who was busy shielding his eyes
Before the tailor could change his mind the deal was done
'Remember,' said the stranger, 'in seven years, I the devil, will come.'

The tailor arrived home to find a slice of bacon and bread for his supper
'I wish there were two rashers of bacon; I'm so hungry,' he muttered,
That was his first wish gone, for there on the plate sizzled another one
'Woman, woman what hast thou done, I wish you were far away from here.'
Terrified, he saw his wife disappear; now he stopped and hesitated in fear
Two wished wasted, he pondered for weeks about what he desired

Now the house grew dirty, he was lonely and tied,
Throwing caution to the wind he exclaimed, "I wish Matty were here."
His third wish now gone, his wife reappeared.

He worked hard and prospered in the next seven years
But now the time had come and it was just as he feared,
With a clap of thunder the devil came forth to claim his prize
The tailor, however, had other things in mind
'I never prospered from the three wishes you cheated me from the start.'
'Come now, you must see that I'm right, where is your heart?'
The devil was angered. 'I will show you that I can fulfil my part
I will grant thee another wish; whatever you ask for will be given
Go on ask for wealth or the topmost pinnacle of thy ambition.'

Glancing around, the tailor saw a dun horse grazing
This gave him an idea that he hoped would save him
'I wish you were riding on yonder horse, back to your quarters
Never to torment me again or anyone else you have in your clutches.'
With a loud roar of rage and fury, the devil was raised into the air
He was placed upon the dun horse which then set off without a care
The tailor stood there in amazement and watched the devil gallop by
'I have won!' he shouted, 'I am free at last!' And ran home to tell his wife
This tale of old Lancashire is known as *The Dule upon Dun*
It took place in a small village near Clitheroe 'round about the year 1821.

Sandra Green

The Game

The referee blows his whistle for the game to commence
James passes the ball to his waiting friend
We stand on the touchline and give our support
And shout well done as the ball is caught
The goalkeeper is good for the opposing side
But so is ours as he runs and dives
Another goal saved and we clap with delight.

It's the second half and no score so far
James passes the ball to his left and
His team mate hits the bar
It bounces back to James who
Takes command of the ball
Dribbles past two players and
Scores the winning goal.

Sandra Green

Time Out

'Dad, we have been training for over an hour
Maybe we should call "Time Out" and go for a shower
I have three games to referee this afternoon
And then I'm in goals playing for the school.'

'You are quite right,' says Dad, 'let's take a rest
After all, you must be at your best.
Don't forget the winner today takes the trophy
Therefore, it's no good you turning up feeling ropey.'

'Well, look who's here, it's Uncle George,
With his daughter, Evelin Rose.'
'Come on, get ready, you kick off at three
In the meantime, I will make a nice cup of tea.'

They enjoy the match, 'We have won! Hurray!'
'You see,' says Dad, 'taking time out helps you play.'
'But, Dad, I don't see how that can be.'
'Well, lad,' says George, 'it was really that Yorkshire cup of tea.'

Sandra Green

Walking Hand in Hand

The sound of leaves rustling
As the wind gently blows
We walk together hand in hand
Enjoying the beauty of autumn
As we talk and make plans
For our retirement days.

Colours of gold, red and brown
Come softly floating down
Holding hands as we stand
And silently look for miles around
What more could we wish for
At this moment in time.

I feel a gentle tug of my hand
As you whisper don't make a sound
For only a short distance away
Is a fox with his nose to the ground
We watch as he lifts his head and sniffs the air
Then dashes into the woods, back to his lair.

We carry on walking along the path
that leads back to our home
Back to the glow of a lovely fire
Where we sit drinking tea and talking for hours
Then the decision is made once and for all
This is definitely the place to stay and retire.

                                                    Sandra Green

Walking in the Lakes

Leaning against the bark of an old oak tree,
Holding my breath as I look at this wondrous sight,
A field of gold stretches before me
Swaying gently, as a swallow takes flight.

Surely, it was a setting similar to this,
And living in the Lake District as he did,
Gave William Wordsworth the inspiration
To write the poem 'Daffodils', of that I am certain.

The old book, I bought in an antique shop, tells of his life
And how Mary Hutchinson became his wife,
It was in his eightieth year that he died,
Amid the surroundings that inspired him,
Grasmere is where his body lies.

It seems like time has stood still,
As I look across the lake to yonder hills,
But alas my holiday is at an end,
Until next year when again
I walk in the Lake District.

Sandra Green

Would You Believe It

'Wake up, Toby, I need you to guard the car
I won't be long, I'm not going far.'
John said that, it must be over an hour ago
And now here comes a man walking very slow
Writing in a book as I began to jump up and down
Well, would you believe it; John is back, about time.

'Please don't give me a ticket I have a blue badge,' says John
Quickly he opens the car door, but this is all wrong
He's taken it from next to his seat and thrown it on the floor
"You bad boy, Toby, you must stop being naughty,' he roared.
He shows it to the traffic warden who nods his head in agreement
Saying, 'You must write and explain the situation.'

Well, would you believe it, blaming innocent me
He had better have bought me a special treat for tea.

                                                    Sandra Green

Wounded

There was a time not so long ago
That my favourite singer felt hurt and wounded deep within
He shed many tears and voiced his fears,
Can such lies be told? He put his life on hold.

Four years fighting evil have gone by,
But God was always on his side,
Now he can rejoice and sing once more,
And like all his fans, 'I thank the Lord.'

                                                        Sandra Green

CPSIA information can be obtained
at www.ICGtesting.com
Printed in the USA
LVHW071725080322
712947LV00018B/580